My Prayers...His Answers

Prayer is the foundation of our relationship with God. It is how we communicate and many times during our intimate moments of prayer, receive revelation and instruction for our lives. Without prayer, the foundation of our relationship with God would crumble. The Bible gives a clear understanding of God's take on prayer, ..."pray without ceasing." Why? Because the Father knows that we must remain in direct communication to receive revelation and instruction for our lives on a daily basis. I pray that as you log your prayers and His answers that you will see the importance of presenting your requests before God and allowing Him to answer. My hope is that as you utilize this journal that you'd get excited about talking to the Father!

-Vonté Boyd

GIFTED TO

Overseer N. Ann McDuffie

FROM

Vontae L Boyd

DATE

August 5, 2018

Emotion Icons

Feeling...

Thankful	Surprised
Blessed	Ecstatic
Favored	Happy
In Awe	Overjoyed
Prosperous	Content

My Prayers...His Answers

Date / Time:
8/8/2017 - 6am

My Prayer for

_____ Peace _____

Lord, I know that your peace surpasses all
understanding. In this situation I'm going
through, I ask you to grant me your peace...In
Jesus name, Amen.

God's Answer

Date / Time:
8/8/2017 - 4:32apm

Peace I leave with you; my peace I give you. I do not
give to you as the world gives. Do not let your hearts be
troubled and do not be afraid. Rest in my peace.

My Prayers...His Answers

Desired Outcome: (Yes)/ No

Scripture: **Hebrews 12:14**

Singing: **Oh, How He Loves Me**

Thankful

Reflections:

As I was driving back to work from lunch, my favorite song came on the radio "Oh, How He Loves Me." I began to cry as the song ministered to me and I was immediately reminded to take solace in the comfort of God. I heard a still small voice reassuring me that He is in control. I felt sudden peace. I am so thankful. Thank you Lord for granting my request.

Date / Time:

My Prayer for

_____

_____
_____
_____
_____
_____
_____
_____

God's Answer   Date / Time:

_____
_____
_____
_____
_____
_____
_____
_____
_____
_____
_____
_____
_____

Desired Outcome: Yes / No

Scripture:

Singing:

Reflections:

_____

_____

_____

_____

_____

_____

_____

_____

_____

_____

_____

_____

_____

_____

_____

_____

_____

_____

_____

Date / Time:

My Prayer for

_____

_____
_____
_____
_____
_____
_____
_____

God's Answer   Date / Time:

_____
_____
_____
_____
_____
_____
_____
_____
_____
_____
_____
_____
_____

Desired Outcome: Yes / No

Scripture:

Singing:

Reflections:

_____

_____

_____

_____

_____

_____

_____

_____

_____

_____

_____

_____

_____

_____

_____

_____

_____

_____

_____

_____

_____

Date / Time:

My Prayer for

_____

_____
_____
_____
_____
_____
_____
_____

God's Answer   Date / Time:

_____
_____
_____
_____
_____
_____
_____
_____
_____
_____
_____
_____

Desired Outcome: Yes / No

Scripture:

Singing:

Reflections:

_____

_____

_____

_____

_____

_____

_____

_____

_____

_____

_____

_____

_____

_____

_____

_____

_____

_____

Date / Time:

My Prayer for

_____

_____
_____
_____
_____
_____
_____
_____

God's Answer   Date / Time:

_____
_____
_____
_____
_____
_____
_____
_____
_____
_____
_____
_____
_____

Desired Outcome: Yes / No

Scripture:

Singing:

Reflections:

_____

_____

_____

_____

_____

_____

_____

_____

_____

_____

_____

_____

_____

_____

_____

_____

_____

_____

Date / Time:

My Prayer for

_____

_____
_____
_____
_____
_____
_____
_____

God's Answer   Date / Time:

_____
_____
_____
_____
_____
_____
_____
_____
_____
_____
_____
_____
_____

Desired Outcome: Yes / No

Scripture:

Singing:

Reflections:

_____
_____
_____
_____
_____
_____
_____
_____
_____
_____
_____
_____
_____
_____
_____
_____
_____
_____

Date / Time:

My Prayer for

_____

_____
_____
_____
_____
_____
_____
_____

God's Answer   Date / Time:

_____
_____
_____
_____
_____
_____
_____
_____
_____
_____
_____
_____
_____

Desired Outcome: Yes / No

Scripture:

Singing:

Reflections:

_____
_____
_____
_____
_____
_____
_____
_____
_____
_____
_____
_____
_____
_____
_____
_____
_____
_____

Date / Time:

My Prayer for

_____

_____
_____
_____
_____
_____
_____
_____

God's Answer   Date / Time:

_____
_____
_____
_____
_____
_____
_____
_____
_____
_____
_____
_____
_____

Desired Outcome: Yes / No

Scripture:

Singing:

Reflections:

_____

_____

_____

_____

_____

_____

_____

_____

_____

_____

_____

_____

_____

_____

_____

_____

_____

_____

_____

_____

Date / Time:

My Prayer for

_____

_____
_____
_____
_____
_____
_____
_____

God's Answer   Date / Time:

_____
_____
_____
_____
_____
_____
_____
_____
_____
_____
_____
_____
_____

Desired Outcome: Yes / No

Scripture:

Singing:

Reflections:

_____

_____

_____

_____

_____

_____

_____

_____

_____

_____

_____

_____

_____

_____

_____

_____

_____

_____

_____

Date / Time:

My Prayer for

_____

_____

_____

_____

_____

_____

_____

God's Answer   Date / Time:

_____

_____

_____

_____

_____

_____

_____

_____

_____

_____

_____

Desired Outcome: Yes / No

Scripture:

Singing:

Reflections:

_____

_____

_____

_____

_____

_____

_____

_____

_____

_____

_____

_____

_____

_____

_____

_____

_____

_____

_____

_____

Date / Time:

My Prayer for

_____

_____
_____
_____
_____
_____
_____
_____
_____

God's Answer   Date / Time:

_____
_____
_____
_____
_____
_____
_____
_____
_____
_____
_____
_____
_____

Desired Outcome: Yes / No

Scripture:

Singing:

Reflections:

_____

_____

_____

_____

_____

_____

_____

_____

_____

_____

_____

_____

_____

_____

_____

_____

_____

_____

My Prayers...His Answers

Date / Time:

My Prayer for

_____

_____
_____
_____
_____
_____
_____
_____

God's Answer   Date / Time:

_____
_____
_____
_____
_____
_____
_____
_____
_____
_____
_____
_____
_____

Desired Outcome: Yes / No

Scripture:

Singing:

Reflections:

_____

_____

_____

_____

_____

_____

_____

_____

_____

_____

_____

_____

_____

_____

_____

_____

_____

_____

Date / Time:

My Prayer for

_____

_____
_____
_____
_____
_____
_____
_____

God's Answer   Date / Time:

_____
_____
_____
_____
_____
_____
_____
_____
_____
_____
_____
_____
_____

Desired Outcome: Yes / No

Scripture:

Singing:

Reflections:

_____

_____

_____

_____

_____

_____

_____

_____

_____

_____

_____

_____

_____

_____

_____

_____

_____

_____

_____

_____

Date / Time:

My Prayer for

_____

_____
_____
_____
_____
_____
_____
_____

God's Answer   Date / Time:

_____
_____
_____
_____
_____
_____
_____
_____
_____
_____
_____
_____
_____

Desired Outcome: Yes / No

Scripture:

Singing:

Reflections:

_____

_____

_____

_____

_____

_____

_____

_____

_____

_____

_____

_____

_____

_____

_____

_____

_____

_____

My Prayers...His Answers

Date / Time:

My Prayer for

_____

_____
_____
_____
_____
_____
_____
_____

God's Answer   Date / Time:

_____
_____
_____
_____
_____
_____
_____
_____
_____
_____
_____
_____

Desired Outcome: Yes / No

Scripture:

Singing:

Reflections:

_____
_____
_____
_____
_____
_____
_____
_____
_____
_____
_____
_____
_____
_____
_____
_____
_____
_____
_____

Date / Time:

My Prayer for

_____

_____
_____
_____
_____
_____
_____
_____

God's Answer   Date / Time:

_____
_____
_____
_____
_____
_____
_____
_____
_____
_____
_____
_____

Desired Outcome: Yes / No

Scripture:

Singing:

Reflections:

_____

_____

_____

_____

_____

_____

_____

_____

_____

_____

_____

_____

_____

_____

_____

_____

_____

_____

_____

Date / Time:

My Prayer for

_____

_____

_____

_____

_____

_____

_____

_____

God's Answer

Date / Time:

_____

_____

_____

_____

_____

_____

_____

_____

_____

_____

_____

_____

Desired Outcome: Yes / No

Scripture:

Singing:

Reflections:

_____

_____

_____

_____

_____

_____

_____

_____

_____

_____

_____

_____

_____

_____

_____

_____

_____

_____

_____

Date / Time:

My Prayer for

_____

_____
_____
_____
_____
_____
_____
_____

God's Answer   Date / Time:

_____
_____
_____
_____
_____
_____
_____
_____
_____
_____
_____
_____
_____
_____

Desired Outcome: Yes / No

Scripture:

Singing:

Reflections:

_____

_____

_____

_____

_____

_____

_____

_____

_____

_____

_____

_____

_____

_____

_____

_____

_____

_____

_____

Date / Time:

My Prayer for

_____

_____
_____
_____
_____
_____
_____
_____

God's Answer   Date / Time:

_____
_____
_____
_____
_____
_____
_____
_____
_____
_____
_____
_____
_____

Desired Outcome: Yes / No

Scripture:

Singing:

Reflections:

_____
_____
_____
_____
_____
_____
_____
_____
_____
_____
_____
_____
_____
_____
_____
_____
_____
_____
_____

My Prayers...His Answers

Date / Time:

My Prayer for

_____

_____
_____
_____
_____
_____
_____
_____

God's Answer   Date / Time:

_____
_____
_____
_____
_____
_____
_____
_____
_____
_____
_____
_____
_____

Desired Outcome: Yes / No

Scripture:

Singing:

Reflections:

Date / Time:

My Prayer for

_____

_____
_____
_____
_____
_____
_____
_____
_____

God's Answer   Date / Time:

_____
_____
_____
_____
_____
_____
_____
_____
_____
_____
_____
_____
_____
_____

Desired Outcome: Yes / No

Scripture:

Singing:

Reflections:

_____

_____

_____

_____

_____

_____

_____

_____

_____

_____

_____

_____

_____

_____

_____

_____

_____

_____

_____

Date / Time:

My Prayer for

_____

_____
_____
_____
_____
_____
_____
_____
_____

God's Answer   Date / Time:

_____
_____
_____
_____
_____
_____
_____
_____
_____
_____
_____
_____
_____
_____

Desired Outcome: Yes / No

Scripture:

Singing:

Reflections:

_____

_____

_____

_____

_____

_____

_____

_____

_____

_____

_____

_____

_____

_____

_____

_____

_____

_____

My Prayers...His Answers

Date / Time:

My Prayer for

_____

_____
_____
_____
_____
_____
_____
_____

God's Answer   Date / Time:

_____
_____
_____
_____
_____
_____
_____
_____
_____
_____
_____
_____

Desired Outcome: Yes / No

Scripture:

Singing:

Reflections:

Date / Time:

My Prayer for

_____

_____
_____
_____
_____
_____
_____
_____

God's Answer   Date / Time:

_____
_____
_____
_____
_____
_____
_____
_____
_____
_____
_____
_____

Desired Outcome: Yes / No

Scripture:

Singing:

Reflections:

_____

_____

_____

_____

_____

_____

_____

_____

_____

_____

_____

_____

_____

_____

_____

_____

_____

_____

_____

Date / Time:

My Prayer for

_____

_____
_____
_____
_____
_____
_____
_____

God's Answer   Date / Time:

_____
_____
_____
_____
_____
_____
_____
_____
_____
_____
_____
_____
_____

Desired Outcome: Yes / No

Scripture:

Singing:

Reflections:

_____

_____

_____

_____

_____

_____

_____

_____

_____

_____

_____

_____

_____

_____

_____

_____

_____

_____

_____

_____

_____

_____

Date / Time:

My Prayer for

_____

_____
_____
_____
_____
_____
_____
_____
_____

God's Answer   Date / Time:

_____
_____
_____
_____
_____
_____
_____
_____
_____
_____
_____
_____
_____

Desired Outcome: Yes / No

Scripture:

Singing:

Reflections:

_____

_____

_____

_____

_____

_____

_____

_____

_____

_____

_____

_____

_____

_____

_____

_____

_____

_____

_____

Date / Time:

My Prayer for

_____

_____
_____
_____
_____
_____
_____
_____

God's Answer   Date / Time:

_____
_____
_____
_____
_____
_____
_____
_____
_____
_____
_____
_____
_____

Desired Outcome: Yes / No

Scripture:

Singing:

Reflections:

_____
_____
_____
_____
_____
_____
_____
_____
_____
_____
_____
_____
_____
_____
_____
_____
_____
_____
_____

My Prayers...His Answers

Date / Time:

My Prayer for

_____

_____
_____
_____
_____
_____
_____
_____

God's Answer   Date / Time:

_____
_____
_____
_____
_____
_____
_____
_____
_____
_____
_____
_____

Desired Outcome: Yes / No

Scripture:

Singing:

Reflections:

My Prayers...His Answers

Date / Time:

My Prayer for

_____

_____
_____
_____
_____
_____
_____
_____
_____

God's Answer   Date / Time:

_____
_____
_____
_____
_____
_____
_____
_____
_____
_____
_____
_____
_____

Desired Outcome: Yes / No

Scripture:

Singing:

Reflections:

_____

_____

_____

_____

_____

_____

_____

_____

_____

_____

_____

_____

_____

_____

_____

_____

_____

_____

_____

Date / Time:

My Prayer for

_____

_____
_____
_____
_____
_____
_____
_____

God's Answer   Date / Time:

_____
_____
_____
_____
_____
_____
_____
_____
_____
_____
_____
_____
_____

Desired Outcome: Yes / No

Scripture:

Singing:

Reflections:

_____

_____

_____

_____

_____

_____

_____

_____

_____

_____

_____

_____

_____

_____

_____

_____

_____

_____

_____

_____

My Prayers...His Answers

Date / Time:

My Prayer for

_____

_____
_____
_____
_____
_____
_____
_____
_____

God's Answer   Date / Time:

_____
_____
_____
_____
_____
_____
_____
_____
_____
_____
_____
_____
_____

Desired Outcome: Yes / No

Scripture:

Singing:

Reflections:

_____
_____
_____
_____
_____
_____
_____
_____
_____
_____
_____
_____
_____
_____
_____
_____
_____
_____
_____

Date / Time:

My Prayer for

_____

_____

_____

_____

_____

_____

_____

_____

God's Answer   Date / Time:

_____

_____

_____

_____

_____

_____

_____

_____

_____

_____

_____

_____

Desired Outcome: Yes / No

Scripture:

Singing:

Reflections:

_____

_____

_____

_____

_____

_____

_____

_____

_____

_____

_____

_____

_____

_____

_____

_____

_____

_____

_____

_____

Date / Time:

My Prayer for

_____

_____
_____
_____
_____
_____
_____
_____

God's Answer   Date / Time:

_____
_____
_____
_____
_____
_____
_____
_____
_____
_____
_____
_____

Desired Outcome: Yes / No

Scripture:

Singing:

Reflections:

_____

_____

_____

_____

_____

_____

_____

_____

_____

_____

_____

_____

_____

_____

_____

_____

_____

_____

_____

_____

Date / Time:

My Prayer for

_____

_____
_____
_____
_____
_____
_____
_____

God's Answer   Date / Time:

_____
_____
_____
_____
_____
_____
_____
_____
_____
_____
_____
_____
_____

Desired Outcome: Yes / No

Scripture:

Singing:

Reflections:

_____

_____

_____

_____

_____

_____

_____

_____

_____

_____

_____

_____

_____

_____

_____

_____

_____

_____

_____

My Prayers...His Answers

Date / Time:

My Prayer for

_____

_____
_____
_____
_____
_____
_____
_____

God's Answer   Date / Time:

_____
_____
_____
_____
_____
_____
_____
_____
_____
_____
_____
_____

Desired Outcome: Yes / No

Scripture:

Singing:

Reflections:

_____

_____

_____

_____

_____

_____

_____

_____

_____

_____

_____

_____

_____

_____

_____

_____

_____

_____

Date / Time:

My Prayer for

_____

_____
_____
_____
_____
_____
_____
_____

God's Answer   Date / Time:

_____
_____
_____
_____
_____
_____
_____
_____
_____
_____
_____
_____
_____

Desired Outcome: Yes / No

Scripture:

Singing:

Reflections:

_____

_____

_____

_____

_____

_____

_____

_____

_____

_____

_____

_____

_____

_____

_____

_____

_____

_____

_____

_____

Date / Time:

My Prayer for

_____

_____
_____
_____
_____
_____
_____
_____

God's Answer   Date / Time:

_____
_____
_____
_____
_____
_____
_____
_____
_____
_____
_____
_____

Desired Outcome: Yes / No

Scripture:

Singing:

Reflections:

_____

_____

_____

_____

_____

_____

_____

_____

_____

_____

_____

_____

_____

_____

_____

_____

_____

_____

_____

_____

Date / Time:

My Prayer for

_____

_____
_____
_____
_____
_____
_____
_____

God's Answer   Date / Time:

_____
_____
_____
_____
_____
_____
_____
_____
_____
_____
_____
_____

Desired Outcome: Yes / No

Scripture:

Singing:

Reflections:

_____

_____

_____

_____

_____

_____

_____

_____

_____

_____

_____

_____

_____

_____

_____

_____

_____

_____

Date / Time:

My Prayer for

_____

_____
_____
_____
_____
_____
_____
_____
_____

God's Answer   Date / Time:

_____
_____
_____
_____
_____
_____
_____
_____
_____
_____
_____
_____

Desired Outcome: Yes / No

Scripture:

Singing:

Reflections:

_____

_____

_____

_____

_____

_____

_____

_____

_____

_____

_____

_____

_____

_____

_____

_____

_____

_____

_____

_____

Date / Time:

My Prayer for

_____

_____

_____

_____

_____

_____

_____

God's Answer   Date / Time:

_____

_____

_____

_____

_____

_____

_____

_____

_____

_____

_____

_____

Desired Outcome: Yes / No

Scripture:

Singing:

Reflections:

_____

_____

_____

_____

_____

_____

_____

_____

_____

_____

_____

_____

_____

_____

_____

_____

_____

_____

Date / Time:

My Prayer for

_____

_____
_____
_____
_____
_____
_____
_____

God's Answer

Date / Time:

_____
_____
_____
_____
_____
_____
_____
_____
_____
_____
_____
_____

Desired Outcome: Yes / No

Scripture:

Singing:

Reflections:

_____

_____

_____

_____

_____

_____

_____

_____

_____

_____

_____

_____

_____

_____

_____

_____

_____

_____

_____

My Prayers...His Answers

Date / Time:

My Prayer for

_____

_____
_____
_____
_____
_____
_____

God's Answer   Date / Time:

_____
_____
_____
_____
_____
_____
_____
_____
_____
_____
_____
_____

Desired Outcome: Yes / No

Scripture:

Singing:

Reflections:

_____

_____

_____

_____

_____

_____

_____

_____

_____

_____

_____

_____

_____

_____

_____

_____

_____

_____

_____

My Prayers...His Answers

Date / Time:

My Prayer for

_____

_____
_____
_____
_____
_____
_____
_____

God's Answer   Date / Time:

_____
_____
_____
_____
_____
_____
_____
_____
_____
_____
_____
_____
_____

Desired Outcome: Yes / No

Scripture:

Singing:

Reflections:

Date / Time:

My Prayer for

_____

_____
_____
_____
_____
_____
_____
_____

God's Answer   Date / Time:

_____
_____
_____
_____
_____
_____
_____
_____
_____
_____
_____
_____
_____

Desired Outcome: Yes / No

Scripture:

Singing:

Reflections:

_____

_____

_____

_____

_____

_____

_____

_____

_____

_____

_____

_____

_____

_____

_____

_____

_____

_____

_____

Date / Time:

My Prayer for

_____

_____
_____
_____
_____
_____
_____
_____

God's Answer

Date / Time:

_____
_____
_____
_____
_____
_____
_____
_____
_____
_____
_____

Desired Outcome: Yes / No

Scripture:

Singing:

Reflections:

_____

_____

_____

_____

_____

_____

_____

_____

_____

_____

_____

_____

_____

_____

_____

_____

_____

_____

_____

Date / Time:

My Prayer for

_____

_____
_____
_____
_____
_____
_____
_____

God's Answer   Date / Time:

_____
_____
_____
_____
_____
_____
_____
_____
_____
_____
_____
_____
_____

Desired Outcome: Yes / No

Scripture:

Singing:

Reflections:

Date / Time:

My Prayer for

_____

_____
_____
_____
_____
_____
_____
_____

God's Answer   Date / Time:

_____
_____
_____
_____
_____
_____
_____
_____
_____
_____
_____
_____
_____

Desired Outcome: Yes / No

Scripture:

Singing:

Reflections:

_____

_____

_____

_____

_____

_____

_____

_____

_____

_____

_____

_____

_____

_____

_____

_____

_____

_____

_____

Date / Time:

My Prayer for

_____

_____
_____
_____
_____
_____
_____
_____

God's Answer

Date / Time:

_____
_____
_____
_____
_____
_____
_____
_____
_____
_____
_____
_____
_____
_____

Desired Outcome: Yes / No

Scripture:

Singing:

Reflections:

_____

_____

_____

_____

_____

_____

_____

_____

_____

_____

_____

_____

_____

_____

_____

_____

_____

_____

Date / Time:

My Prayer for

_____

_____
_____
_____
_____
_____
_____
_____

God's Answer   Date / Time:

_____
_____
_____
_____
_____
_____
_____
_____
_____
_____
_____
_____
_____

Desired Outcome: Yes / No

Scripture:

Singing:

Reflections:

_____

_____

_____

_____

_____

_____

_____

_____

_____

_____

_____

_____

_____

_____

_____

_____

_____

_____

_____

My Prayers...His Answers

Date / Time:

My Prayer for

_____

_____
_____
_____
_____
_____
_____
_____
_____

God's Answer   Date / Time:

_____
_____
_____
_____
_____
_____
_____
_____
_____
_____
_____
_____
_____

Desired Outcome: Yes / No

Scripture:

Singing:

Reflections:

_____

_____

_____

_____

_____

_____

_____

_____

_____

_____

_____

_____

_____

_____

_____

_____

_____

Date / Time:

My Prayer for

_____

_____
_____
_____
_____
_____
_____
_____

God's Answer   Date / Time:

_____
_____
_____
_____
_____
_____
_____
_____
_____
_____
_____
_____
_____

99

Desired Outcome: Yes / No

Scripture:

Singing:

Reflections:

Date / Time:

My Prayer for

_____

_____
_____
_____
_____
_____
_____

God's Answer   Date / Time:

_____
_____
_____
_____
_____
_____
_____
_____
_____
_____
_____
_____

Desired Outcome: Yes / No

Scripture:

Singing:

Reflections:

_____

_____

_____

_____

_____

_____

_____

_____

_____

_____

_____

_____

_____

_____

_____

_____

_____

_____

My Prayers...His Answers

Date / Time:

My Prayer for

_____

_____
_____
_____
_____
_____
_____
_____
_____

God's Answer

Date / Time:

_____
_____
_____
_____
_____
_____
_____
_____
_____
_____
_____
_____
_____
_____
_____

Desired Outcome: Yes / No

Scripture:

Singing:

Reflections:

_____

_____

_____

_____

_____

_____

_____

_____

_____

_____

_____

_____

_____

_____

_____

_____

_____

_____

My Prayers...His Answers

Date / Time:

My Prayer for

_____

_____
_____
_____
_____
_____
_____
_____

God's Answer

Date / Time:

_____
_____
_____
_____
_____
_____
_____
_____
_____
_____
_____
_____

105

Desired Outcome: Yes / No

Scripture:

Singing:

Reflections:

_____

_____

_____

_____

_____

_____

_____

_____

_____

_____

_____

_____

_____

_____

_____

_____

_____

_____

Date / Time:

My Prayer for

_____

_____
_____
_____
_____
_____
_____
_____

God's Answer   Date / Time:

_____
_____
_____
_____
_____
_____
_____
_____
_____
_____
_____
_____

Desired Outcome: Yes / No

Scripture:

Singing:

Reflections:

_____

_____

_____

_____

_____

_____

_____

_____

_____

_____

_____

_____

_____

_____

_____

_____

_____

_____

My Prayers...His Answers

Date / Time:

My Prayer for

_____

_____
_____
_____
_____
_____
_____
_____

God's Answer   Date / Time:

_____
_____
_____
_____
_____
_____
_____
_____
_____
_____
_____
_____
_____

Desired Outcome: Yes / No

Scripture:

Singing:

Reflections:

Date / Time:

My Prayer for

_____

_____
_____
_____
_____
_____
_____
_____
_____

God's Answer

Date / Time:

_____
_____
_____
_____
_____
_____
_____
_____
_____
_____
_____
_____
_____
_____

Desired Outcome: Yes / No

Scripture:

Singing:

Reflections:

_____

_____

_____

_____

_____

_____

_____

_____

_____

_____

_____

_____

_____

_____

_____

_____

_____

_____

_____

Date / Time:

My Prayer for

_____

_____
_____
_____
_____
_____
_____
_____

God's Answer   Date / Time:

_____
_____
_____
_____
_____
_____
_____
_____
_____
_____
_____
_____

Desired Outcome: Yes / No

Scripture:

Singing:

Reflections:

_____

_____

_____

_____

_____

_____

_____

_____

_____

_____

_____

_____

_____

_____

_____

_____

_____

_____

Date / Time:

My Prayer for

_____

_____
_____
_____
_____
_____
_____
_____

God's Answer

Date / Time:

_____
_____
_____
_____
_____
_____
_____
_____
_____
_____
_____
_____
_____
_____

Desired Outcome: Yes / No

Scripture:

Singing:

Reflections:

My Prayers...His Answers

Date / Time:

My Prayer for

_____

_____
_____
_____
_____
_____
_____
_____

God's Answer   Date / Time:

_____
_____
_____
_____
_____
_____
_____
_____
_____
_____
_____
_____
_____

Desired Outcome: Yes / No

Scripture:

Singing:

Reflections:

_____
_____
_____
_____
_____
_____
_____
_____
_____
_____
_____
_____
_____
_____
_____
_____
_____
_____
_____

My Prayers...His Answers

Date / Time:

My Prayer for

_____

_____
_____
_____
_____
_____
_____
_____

God's Answer   Date / Time:

_____
_____
_____
_____
_____
_____
_____
_____
_____
_____
_____
_____

Desired Outcome: Yes / No

Scripture:

Singing:

Reflections:

_____

_____

_____

_____

_____

_____

_____

_____

_____

_____

_____

_____

_____

_____

_____

_____

_____

_____

Date / Time:

My Prayer for

_____

_____
_____
_____
_____
_____
_____
_____

God's Answer   Date / Time:

_____
_____
_____
_____
_____
_____
_____
_____
_____
_____
_____
_____

Desired Outcome: Yes / No

Scripture:

Singing:

Reflections:

_____

_____

_____

_____

_____

_____

_____

_____

_____

_____

_____

_____

_____

_____

_____

_____

_____

_____

_____

_____

Date / Time:

My Prayer for

_____

_____

_____

_____

_____

_____

_____

_____

_____

God's Answer

Date / Time:

_____

_____

_____

_____

_____

_____

_____

_____

_____

_____

_____

_____

_____

Desired Outcome: Yes / No

Scripture:

Singing:

Reflections:

_____
_____
_____
_____
_____
_____
_____
_____
_____
_____
_____
_____
_____
_____
_____
_____
_____
_____

Date / Time:

My Prayer for

_____

_____

_____

_____

_____

_____

_____

_____

God's Answer   Date / Time:

_____

_____

_____

_____

_____

_____

_____

_____

_____

_____

_____

_____

_____

_____

Desired Outcome: Yes / No

Scripture:

Singing:

Reflections:

_____

_____

_____

_____

_____

_____

_____

_____

_____

_____

_____

_____

_____

_____

_____

_____

_____

_____

_____

Date / Time:

My Prayer for

_____

_____
_____
_____
_____
_____
_____

God's Answer

Date / Time:

_____
_____
_____
_____
_____
_____
_____
_____
_____
_____
_____
_____

Desired Outcome: Yes / No

Scripture:

Singing:

Reflections:

_____

_____

_____

_____

_____

_____

_____

_____

_____

_____

_____

_____

_____

_____

_____

_____

_____

_____

_____

My Prayers...His Answers

Date / Time:

My Prayer for

_____

_____
_____
_____
_____
_____
_____
_____

God's Answer   Date / Time:

_____
_____
_____
_____
_____
_____
_____
_____
_____
_____
_____
_____
_____

Desired Outcome: Yes / No

Scripture:

Singing:

Reflections:

_____

_____

_____

_____

_____

_____

_____

_____

_____

_____

_____

_____

_____

_____

_____

_____

_____

_____

_____

Date / Time:

My Prayer for

_____

_____
_____
_____
_____
_____
_____
_____

God's Answer   Date / Time:

_____
_____
_____
_____
_____
_____
_____
_____
_____
_____
_____
_____
_____

Desired Outcome: Yes / No

Scripture:

Singing:

Reflections:

_____

_____

_____

_____

_____

_____

_____

_____

_____

_____

_____

_____

_____

_____

_____

_____

_____

_____

Date / Time:

My Prayer for

_____

_____
_____
_____
_____
_____
_____
_____

God's Answer

Date / Time:

_____
_____
_____
_____
_____
_____
_____
_____
_____
_____
_____
_____

Desired Outcome: Yes / No

Scripture:

Singing:

Reflections:

_____

_____

_____

_____

_____

_____

_____

_____

_____

_____

_____

_____

_____

_____

_____

_____

_____

_____

_____

Date / Time:

My Prayer for

_____

_____
_____
_____
_____
_____
_____
_____
_____

God's Answer   Date / Time:

_____
_____
_____
_____
_____
_____
_____
_____
_____
_____
_____
_____
_____
_____

Desired Outcome: Yes / No

Scripture:

Singing:

Reflections:

Date / Time:

My Prayer for

_____

_____
_____
_____
_____
_____
_____
_____

God's Answer   Date / Time:

_____
_____
_____
_____
_____
_____
_____
_____
_____
_____
_____
_____

Desired Outcome: Yes / No

Scripture:

Singing:

Reflections:

_____

_____

_____

_____

_____

_____

_____

_____

_____

_____

_____

_____

_____

_____

_____

_____

_____

_____

_____

Date / Time:

My Prayer for

_____

_____

_____

_____

_____

_____

_____

_____

God's Answer   Date / Time:

_____

_____

_____

_____

_____

_____

_____

_____

_____

_____

_____

_____

Desired Outcome: Yes / No

Scripture:

Singing:

Reflections:

Date / Time:

My Prayer for

_____

_____
_____
_____
_____
_____
_____
_____

God's Answer   Date / Time:

_____
_____
_____
_____
_____
_____
_____
_____
_____
_____
_____
_____
_____
_____

Desired Outcome: Yes / No

Scripture:

Singing:

Reflections:

_____

_____

_____

_____

_____

_____

_____

_____

_____

_____

_____

_____

_____

_____

_____

_____

_____

_____

My Prayers...His Answers

Date / Time:

My Prayer for

_____

_____
_____
_____
_____
_____
_____
_____
_____

God's Answer   Date / Time:

_____
_____
_____
_____
_____
_____
_____
_____
_____
_____
_____
_____
_____

Desired Outcome: Yes / No

Scripture:

Singing:

Reflections:

_____

_____

_____

_____

_____

_____

_____

_____

_____

_____

_____

_____

_____

_____

_____

_____

_____

_____

Notes
(Corresponding page: _____)

Notes
(Corresponding page: _____)

Notes
(Corresponding page: _____)

_____

_____

_____

_____

_____

_____

_____

_____

_____

_____

_____

_____

_____

_____

_____

_____

_____

_____

_____

_____

_____

_____

_____

_____

_____

_____

_____

_____

_____

Notes
(Corresponding page: _____)

Notes
(Corresponding page: _____)

Notes
(Corresponding page: _____)

Notes
(Corresponding page: _____)

Notes
(Corresponding page: _____)

Notes
(Corresponding page: _____)

Notes
(Corresponding page: _____)

Notes
(Corresponding page: _____)

94435655R00090

Made in the USA
Lexington, KY
29 July 2018